Water Polo Basics: All About Water Polo

ISBN-13: 978-1480026483
ISBN-10: 1480026484

Copyright Notice

WATER POLO BASICS: ALL ABOUT WATER POLO

Gareth Balline

I dedicate this to the lucky people who've been touched by the fun and excitement of water polo...

Contents

Water Polo:
A Brief History

Water polo was known in the past as a rough and brutal sport, but the modern version of the game is actually a lot more genteel in comparison.

The game was first developed in England sometime in the mid-1800s as a new version of rugby.

People played it in indoor pools as well as outdoors in ponds and lakes.

In 1870, rules for indoor water polo were drafted by the London Swimming Association.

Among other things, these rules awarded a goal to a team each time a player successfully tags the far wall using two hands to hold the ball.

Goalies at the time were allowed to wait by the poolside and then jump onto players trying to score a goal.

No wonder the games were brutal in those days.

The Scots were the first to utilize cage goals for the sport and they modified the game to resemble soccer more than rugby.

They also placed more emphasis on passing and employed a bigger ball.

In 1889, the Scottish rules, which were a lot more civilized than the original rules, were adopted by Hungary.

Austria and Germany followed suit in 1894, France did so in 1895, and Belgium also adopted the new rules in 1900.

Meanwhile, the original brutal version was flourishing in the United States.

Water polo gained even more popularity as it became the very first team sport to be included in the Olympic Games in 1900.

The inherent violence of the game limited it to men's events. And because of the preference of the U.S. for the more brutal version, many European teams chose not to participate in the sport during the 1904 Olympics held in the country.

The very first women's game was played in 1906 in Holland, but it only gained considerable popularity almost a hundred years later.

It was, in fact, practically abandoned during the 1960s.

When a Hungarian water polo coach introduced the dry pass in 1928, the dynamics of the game were forever changed.

This development resulted in a Hungarian dynasty in the sport that spanned sixty years.

Because of the emphasis on passing, players had to develop both skill and finesse, since brute force no longer sufficed.

In 1930, FINA was established as the official rule-making and governing body for the sport.

This was when the U.S. clubs that still played under the original rules finally switched to the less violent version of the sport.

In 1949, another rule change sped up game play and in the 1970s, water polo started using the shot clock.

Women's water polo started to gain considerable popularity after the 1960s.
This popularity continued growing and the sport is now played in a lot of American high schools.

It is said to be just as rough as the men's version. The United States team won the very first FINA World Cup for Women in 1979.

The event finally became an Olympic game in 2000, after it was introduced as a demonstration sport in the 1996 Olympics.

Water Polo Rules

Water polo is the very first team sport to have been included in the Olympic Games.

It's the kind of sport that requires players to develop a dual set of skills.

The first skill is that of swimming and the second is that of developing good judgement and a keen eye for spotting the ball.

Water polo is a team sport played in a pool with netted goals set up at both ends.

The two competing teams will attempt to score goals by shooting the ball into their opponent's goal. One goal is equivalent to one point.

For men's competitions, the playing area has to be at least 20 meters wide and as much as 30 meters long, with an average depth of 1.8 meters.

For women's competitions, the playing area is generally 17 meters wide and 25 meters long.

A water polo ball looks like a soccer ball, weighs around 400g-450g, and has a circumference of 68cm-71cm.

It has about the same size as a volleyball.

The goals used in the sport typically feature a wooden, metal, or plastic frame and has the ability to float on water.

Each of the goals has to be 3 meters wide, 30cm deep, and 90cm high from the surface to the top of its frame.

Each team in water polo has seven players, with six field players and one goalkeeper.

The field players strive to score goals while the goalkeeper strives to prevent the other team from scoring.

Each team is also allowed to have six substitute players waiting on the sidelines.

All field players are required to handle the ball with only one hand, while the goalkeeper gets to handle it with both hands.

All players are required to remain afloat during game play. This is why plenty of substitutes are needed, since treading water can be very tiresome.

The official rules also call for the home team to wear blue caps while the visiting team wears white caps.

Goalkeepers are the only players who get to wear red caps.

There are four periods in the game with seven minutes each and a two-minute interval in between.

As opposed to collegiate and Olympic water polo matches, each period in club leagues lasts for only five minutes.

The game play in water polo resembles soccer and handball, although the common use of power plays has resulted in the game being likened to ice hockey.

Just like many other water sports, the primary goal in water polo is to move the ball from the center of the playing area to the opposing team's goal.

Each team is given only thirty seconds to attempt a goal. When the allotted time has passed without an attempt, possession is awarded to the other team.

Only the team that has possession of the ball gets to call a timeout. There are two one-minute timeouts allotted to each team.

The team with the most number of points upon completion of the four periods wins the game. Other than the players, a match also requires two goal judges, two referees, two recorders, and two timekeepers.

Water Polo Gear

Compared to other athletes, water polo players don't really need much gear.

They basically just need a wetsuit, a swimming cap, and a ball in order to get a water polo game going.

Of course, you'll have to find a place to play in – a pool, pond, or lake should do.

Following is a quick guide on the individual water polo gear you'll need.

Suits

Naturally, you'll need a swimsuit if you're going to play a water sport. The most important thing to remember as regards your suit is that it has to have a comfortably snug fit.

This means it should fit tight, but still allow you to freely stretch, twist, and turn for the duration of the game.

Take note that practice suits often differ from game suits, but the style of these two suits is generally the same.

Suits for women are typically one-piece suits that cover the whole torso. They're designed for minimum drag and for giving opposing players as few places to grab as possible. These suits therefore feature zippers rather than Y straps.

Male players are generally required to wear swimming trunks or briefs, as these allow them to move freely in the water.

As opposed to women's swimwear, these cover only the groin, hips, and buttocks.

Longer suits that extend down the thighs typically make movement a lot more difficult because of the added drag and aren't really advisable for water polo.

Swimming Caps

Anyone who wants to play water polo and sports hair that goes past their shoulders should definitely invest in at least two swimming caps. It doesn't really matter much if you choose latex or silicone caps.

What matters most is that you're able to keep your hair away from your face and out of the grasp of opposing players.

And since water polo matches typically require home teams to wear white caps and visiting teams to wear blue caps, it's a good idea to buy a cap in each color.

Take note that caps used for water polo differ from regular swimming caps because they're typically equipped with ear guards and chin straps.

Players' numbers are also typically displayed on their caps. The good thing is that most water polo teams provide their players with matching practice and game caps.

Balls

Water polo balls for men are measured as Size 5, with a circumference of around 68 to 71 centimeters.

Balls used for women's matches are a Size 4, with a circumference of 65 to 67 centimeters.

And balls used by younger players are known as junior-sized balls. Water polo balls generally weigh around 400 to 450 grams.

They're traditionally colored yellow, although the latest matches have featured three colors in wave designs.

These days, it's normal to see water polo balls with colored sections or of different colors. The exterior of these balls is rubber and it is designed specifically for better grip in wet conditions.

Other than the basic water polo gear, you can also choose to make use of accessories like a pair of especially-designed eye shields and a mouth guard to keep your mouth area safe from wayward elbows and balls.

The fact that you don't need much gear to play water polo makes it extremely important to make sure you invest only in items of excellent quality.

Conditioning

Following is a comprehensive guide to conditioning for water polo.

Take note that the conditioning program required for this sport isn't something you can take lightly.

The sport itself is quite intense, so you need some intensive conditioning as well in order to become any good at water polo.

You have the option of undergoing this program for as long as you want, but the general advice is to perform the workouts for at least 12 weeks before adding a little variety.

The conditioning program described herein is comprised of nine workouts that need to be cycled on a 3-days-on/1-day-off manner.

You'll have to rework your cycling around your skills training sessions and game days, of course.

Workout #1:

The first workout needs to be done in a pool. It involves the act of throwing a water polo ball as far as you can and then swimming after it.

Keep repeating the process until you've swum for a total of 3.5 kilometers. Time yourself while performing the exercise and then try to improve your time for every session.

Workout #2:

The second workout works for both strength and general conditioning. You need to perform three sets of deep front squats with 15 repetitions per set. After this, you need to do three sets of single leg calf raises with 15 repetitions for each leg in one set.

You then have to perform two sets of a bent-over row superset with pull-ups with 10-15 repetitions per set. The next exercise in this workout is three sets of push-ups max. Finally, you need to do two sets of overhead dumbbell presses with 12 repetitions per set.

Workout #3:

The third workout is best performed with a partner. Have your partner stand by the pool's edge with a whistle.

Each time he blows his whistle, he should point in any direction he pleases and then you should swim in that direction until you hear the whistle again.

This workout is best done in five rounds with five minutes per round and a one-minute rest period between rounds.

Workout #4:

The first exercise in the fourth workout is three sets of single leg squats with 12 repetitions per set followed by three sets of clap push-ups with 8 repetitions per set. You then have to do three sets of power cleans with 5 repetitions per set and 50 body weight squats.

Workout #5:

For this workout, you need to do egg beaters for about 30 seconds with your hand raised and then continue for one minute with your hands assisting. Finally, you need to swim underwater as far as you can go. Repeat the process and do the workout repeatedly for 20 minutes.

Workout #6:

This workout involves doing give sets of heavy barbell thrusts with five repetitions per set.

Workout #7:

This workout requires the use of an indoor rower. Row for 100 meters in five sets with 20-second intervals. Row for 250 meters in two sets with 40-second intervals. Row for 500 meters and then row for 1500 meters. Rest for two minutes after each exercises and be sure to row as quickly and as hard as you can.

Workout #8:

This workout begins with three sets of extra slow overhead squats with eight repetitions per set. This is followed by eight repetitions of barbell snatch and then two sets each of extra slow chin-ups and extra slow push-ups max.

Workout #9:

For this workout, you need to swim backstroke for ten meters.

Ask a partner to pass you the ball. Pass the ball back and then swim backstroke for another ten meters.

Repeat the process until you complete 50 meters. Do the same with the freestyle stroke.

Complete three sets with a two-minute rest between sets.

Do the egg beater with hands up for 30 seconds and then with hands assisting for another 30 seconds. Repeat the process for three minutes.

Fitness for Water Polo

—

If you want to become an excellent water polo player, then you'll have to be effective in multitasking.

Remember that the sport requires you not only to battle the opposing players, but also to keep yourself afloat and to move in the right direction at all times.

Doing all these things at once requires both coordination and strength. Regular workouts should therefore be an integral part of your water polo training.

Bodyweight Workouts

Body weight workouts can be very effective even if they don't involve extra resistance. Although you can probably develop raw strength more effectively with heavy weights, body weight exercises are very effective for developing muscular endurance.

For water polo training, presses, squats, and pull-ups are said to be very effective body weight exercises.

A workout comprised of these exercises may seem too simplistic, but it's actually quite challenging.

You may want to do five repetitions of each exercise and then increase to ten repetitions and so on until your reach 25 repetitions each, after which you should reverse the process and move gradually back down to five repetitions.

Shoulder Workouts

Water polo players often suffer from shoulder injuries, owing to the nature of the game. This is why it's crucial for you to build shoulder strength.

Not only will this help you avoid injury, but it will also enable you to shoot the ball much harder. It's a good idea to set aside one day each work for your shoulder workout session.

The most effective shoulder workout for water polo involves three of lateral dumbbell side raises with 12 repetitions per set, three sets of military press with 12 repetitions per set, four sets of barbell shrugs with 10 repetitions per set, and three sets of reverse fly with eight repetitions per set.

Leg Workouts

Enhancing your leg strength should also be one of your priorities if you want to do well in water polo. Developing leg strength and muscular endurance enables you to move without much difficulty for the duration of a game. Moderate weight training with high repetitions is the best way to enhance muscular endurance.

Experts believe the best leg workout for water polo players involves bicycling and stair running, along with weight training. Medium weights are recommended muscle-building in your legs. The best exercises you can include in this workout are leg presses, leg extensions, squats, and lunges.

Swimming Workout

Naturally, you need to enhance your swimming skills to achieve success in water polo.

And because the sport requires great bursts of speed, you'll certainly benefit from interval training.

Experts recommend incorporating a 12.5 sprint into your workout sessions. Freestyle laps and egg beater kicks are also advised, but you may also incorporate other strokes into your swimming workout to challenge all your muscle groups.

A good routine to follow involves doing a 50-meter freestyle followed by a 12.5-meter sprint and then 20 seconds of egg beater kicks.

Next, you should do a 50-meter freestyle, a 12.5-meter sprint, and then 15 seconds of egg beater kicks.

The next set is a 25-meter freestyle, a 12.5-meter sprint, and 10 seconds of egg beaters. Finally, you should do a 25-meter freestyle and a 12.5-meter sprint. You may repeat the pattern as much as you want.

By incorporating all of the above workouts into your water polo training routine, you should be able to look forward to achieving success in the sport very soon.

Basic Water Polo Drills

Water polo drills designed for beginners can be described simply as a simplified version of the drills designed for pros.

After all, the basics of the game don't change regardless of the players' level of skill or the type of league you play in.

The biggest difference is that beginners still need to learn the fundamentals of the game whereas the pros need to reinforce those fundamentals.

Here are some basic drills for beginners in the sport of water polo:

1. Dribbling

A lot of beginners in water polo fail to recognize the value of good dribbling. Like many others, you could easily make the mistake of thinking that passing is the only way to successfully advance the ball.

The truth is that dribbling is just as important for ball advancement. This drill should help you learn how to swim and handle the ball at the same time.

What you need to do is swim freestyle with the ball in front. Remember to keep your head above the water and let the ball ride on your shoulder. Swim the length of the pool to complete the drill.

2. Dribbling Spin

Another basic skill you need to develop for water polo is ball control. This drill should help you learn how to control the ball while spinning to shoot or pass it.

Starting from backstroke position, you should cradle the ball to move it in your wake. You should then stop, take hold of the ball, and then spin to shoot the ball or pass it to your teammate as instructed. Try to complete the drill as quickly as you can.

3. Short Passing

Passing is another key component in water polo. This drill necessarily requires the participation of the entire team. The aim is for you to advance the ball without delay or any drops. Players should be positioned diagonally down the pool's length about five yards apart.

The first player needs to pass the ball on to the second player and so on until the last player gets the ball and shoots it into the goal. The ball is then passed in the other direction.

4. Shoulder Wrestle

As you know, strength plays a huge role in water polo, which makes this drill ideal for the sport. It requires two players and can be an excellent and fun way to build the strength of your back and leg muscles.

Each player places one hand on the other player's shoulder. You should then start pushing each other down, with the intention of submerging the other player.

The player who succeeds in submerging the other is declared the winner. You may decide beforehand how many rounds you'll be playing and what the winner's reward will be.

The more you perform these drills, the easier it will be for you to master the fundamentals of water polo.

When you're finally able to accomplish the basic movements of the game without having to think too long about the move you're about to make, that's when you can start practicing more advanced drills.

Swimming Drills

Water polo players are often described as swimmers out looking for fun. There may be a bit of truth to that statement, if only for the fact that swimming is the most fundamental skill you need to master in order to become a good water polo player.

Take note, though, that there are important differences between the strokes of lap swimmers and water polo players.

Swimming drills for water polo simulate the quick pace and back-and-forth nature of an actual game, which lap swimming could never mimic.

Here are some of the best swimming drills you can perform to enhance your game in water polo:

1. Lines

This drill helps you improve your ability to swim freestyle with your head up as well as your ability to quickly change directions. Three to seven points should be marked along the pool's length, with each mark at least five feet from the following mark.

Swim freestyle with your head up from one end to the first mark and then turn around to swim back to the starting point.

Once you get to the starting point, you should swim back until you get to the second mark, where you turn and swim back to the starting point again. This goes on until you've approached all of the marks.

2. Sprints/Sprint Tournament

Performing sprints as part of your warm-up session is an excellent way of getting yourself loose. Your team should line up on one end of the pool and then perform at least four sprints each.

Your sprints may include regular freestyle, heads-up freestyles, heads-up freestyle with ball, and heads-up backstroke.

In a sprint tournament, the player who gets to the other end first gets to rest while the others need to do another sprint. The tournament goes on until only two players are left in the pool.

3. Swim and Kicking Sets

Early in the season, you'll likely be advised to focus on conditioning to make sure you're in excellent shape for an actual match. This often involves long-distance swimming and kicking sets.

The length of the sets you perform largely depends on your age and level of experience in the sport. The extra muscle you build through these exercises will also help you avoid injury.

Shorter versions of the sets may also be used to increase your speed and promote explosive power. It's best to use different swimming strokes so as to avoid repetitive use injury.

4. Heads-up Progression

This drill helps improve your endurance and agility, but should only be done once you've mastered heads-up freestyle swimming. The drill can also add new dimensions to your freestyle stroke. Each exercise in the drill should be done for a lap or two and the entire drill may be repeated as many times as you can.

The drill includes the regular heads-up stroke, heads-up freestyle with elbows held high and a shorter pull as well as a faster stroke.

The next stroke is heads-up freestyle with exaggerated kick and then with a ball and finally with eggbeater. Be sure to keep your head still and always facing forward.

As long as you commit to your regular swimming routine, you should see significant improvements in your stroke, your speed, and your overall game pretty soon.

Passing Drills

Quick and accurate passes are extremely important in water polo, which is why you should strive to master it.

Regardless of whether you're a beginner or an experienced water polo player, you need to maintain good passing practices at all times.

Following are some drills that will help you work on the various aspects of passing. The more variety you use in practice, the better-rounded you become as a player.

1. Passing Distance Drills

You need to learn how to pass accurately both for short and long distances. For that you need strength in your shoulders and arms as well as the proper form and lots of practice.

One of the most effective drills for developing precise long-distance passing involves dry passing with a practice buddy at a five-foot distance.

After making 20 consecutive passes, you should add three feet to the distance and then make 20 more passes.

Add a couple of feet to the distance again and keep repeating the process until you're positioned at the opposite ends of the pool.

You may not be able to successfully throw the ball towards the other end at first, but with enough practice, your distance throwing is sure to improve.

2. Wet Passing Drills

When you play water polo, you'll likely be required to make wet passes as well, so it's just as important to master this skill along with dry passing. One drill that effectively enhances your wet passing skills involves passing wet shots to a practice buddy.

With each pass, the ball should end up about an arm's length from your partner or nearer. When it's your turn to receive, be sure to pick up the ball on the bounce as quickly as you can.

Wet shots don't really require much power, but you need to develop the skill of passing such that the ball doesn't skip or bounce as it lands.

3. Drills for Dexterity

In order for you to develop the ability to pass in different ways, you'll have to get a good feel for the ball.

One drill that can help you achieve this purpose involves passing the ball to your practice buddy's weak side and then receiving it from your weak side as well.

Since this kind of pass is a bit more awkward than receiving from your strong side, you'll have to position your hips properly to absorb the pass.

You torso should be perpendicular to your practice buddy and your strong side should face away from him. It would even be better to perform the drill with two or three other people.

Regardless of what drill you're performing, always remember that a good pass comes from a player who employs proper body positioning and a stable eggbeater.

Furthermore, good passes only happen once you've developed accuracy. The drills discussed above will surely provide you with the necessary skills for good passing in a water polo match.

As always, practice is the key to perfection, so be sure to set a regular schedule for your passing drills.

Shooting Drills

In most cases, a water polo practice session will start with swim sets and then followed by leg work, passing drills, and finally shooting drills.

The shooting drills are important for enhancing your shooting techniques and scoring abilities, of course.

Even goalkeepers benefit from these drills because they serve as excellent warm-up exercises for the arms and legs.

Here are a few simple yet effective shooting drills for both fielders and goalkeepers:

1. **Rear-backs**

This drill is an excellent way for warming up goalkeepers, shooters, and the hole set alike. The drill begins with the hole set positioned in front of the goal.

The other players will then form a line from the five-meter mark fronting the goal.

Each of the players in the line should be holding a ball. The player at the head of the line delivers a wet pass to the hole set and then drives to the goal as soon as he releases the ball.

He should pop up quickly at the three- or four-meter mark and then call for the ball, receive the pass, and take the shot. The process is repeated until all players in the line get to shoot.

2. Two Lines

This drill enhances your passing skills and promotes quick reactive shots. It can be an excellent warm-up drill for both the goalkeeper and field players.

Your team should form two lines at the posts, with one of the lines a bit outside the five-meter mark.

All of the players should have a ball. The player at the head of the line pump fakes a couple of times and then passes the ball to the player at the head of the other line.

The player receiving the pass will then shoot the ball and go to the back of the line.

The player who first passed the ball will then become the receiver and shooter on the next pass. The drill continues until all player have taken their turn at shooting.

3. Triangle

This drill incorporates swimming, passing, and shooting. It begins with three players positioned in a triangle fronting the goal. There should be one player at each post and then a third player at point position.

The other players then line up at point position with a ball in hand. The first player at point position starts the drill by passing the ball to the player on his left, who then passes it across to the player at the other post.

This player will then pass the ball back to the player at point position, after which the point position player shoots and they rotate clockwise.

The last player who passed then goes to the back of the line and the process is repeated until all players have taken their turn at shooting.

4. Perimeter Shooting

This drill helps you develop the ability to shoot from just about every perimeter position. To execute, you team should form a semi-circle fronting the cage, with each player holding a ball.

The player at one post starts the drill by taking a shot, after which the player to his right shoots.

The process continues until all players have taken a turn at shooting. The players then move one position to the left and then repeat the process. The drill goes on until each player has taken a shot from all positions.

These basic drills should help you develop good shooting technique. You can incorporate them into your practice as much as you want in order to strengthen your shooting skills.

Handling Drills

Ball handling skills for water polo are best developed by spending considerable time doing passing and shooting drills as well as scrimmaging with your teammates.

There are also a number of exercises specifically designed to help you improve your ball handling skills quickly.

As a beginner, you'd do well to perform drills that allow you to master the most basic ball handling skills.

Remember that these drills require you to have considerable space as well as a ball of your own.

1. Around the World

To perform this drill, you need to tread as high as you can and then pass the ball around your torso with both hands before you drop back down.

This helps you control the ball even without looking at it and conditions your legs as well. You can choose to do this drill for a set number of passes or a specific amount of time.

2. Ball Bouncing

Pick the ball up, put it back down, and then pick it up again. Do this in different ways for about 30 seconds. Make sure you have full control of the ball at all times.

Your movements may include pressing the ball down and then lifting it up, making it bounce and then catching it on the bounce, pressing it down and then sweeping it into your other hand, and kicking the ball into your hand.

3. Ball Transfers

To begin this drill, you need to hold the ball in throwing position. You should then sweep the ball in front of you and transfer it to your other hand. You should then swing your hand up over your head into throwing position.

Make sure your transfers are smooth and that the ball moves from one hand to the other in a single uninterrupted movement. Continue the drill for a specified amount of time.

4. Spins and Wheels

This drill involves spinning around with a ball in hand. It can challenge your sense of balance and leg strength. You need to pick the ball up, hold your arms out, and then spin in a counter clockwise direction.

After completing one revolution, you need to set the ball down and then repeat the process. Be sure to keep your torso high and upright, and your elbows above the water surface. Continue the drill for 30 seconds or more.

5. Squeeze the Banana

For this drill, you need to simultaneously do eggbeaters while squeezing with the fingertips of one of your hands. With the squeezing motion, launch the ball into the air and then catch it with your other hand. Repeat the process for a predetermined amount of time.

Picking up the ball, throwing it, and catching it may all seem so simple, but doing all these while keeping yourself afloat and in control in a water polo game can be very challenging.

The water surface, the manner in which the ball bounces, and the presence of the opposing players all make it quite difficult to execute smooth pick-ups and accurate passes.

Familiarizing the different ways of picking the ball up and preparing for a shot or a pass is just the first step towards gaining full control of the ball.

And even when you've gained more experience in the sport, you should always remember that your ball handling skills can and should always be improved.

Leg Strength Drills

Your legs are sure to get lots of exercise when you engage in water polo practice, but it's still advisable to add dry land exercises to your routine so you can target specific muscle groups and enhance specific skills, which may be a bit difficult to do in water.

In most cases, certain areas of a water polo player's body become weak in comparison to other areas.

The purpose of dry land training is to focus on those weaker muscle groups. Here are some of the most beneficial leg strength drills for water polo players:

1. Squats

This is one of the most effective all-around exercises for leg strength. They work several muscles when done properly and are among the best calorie-burning exercises as well.

Start with your legs positioned a bit wider than a hip-width apart. Squat until your legs are at a 90-degree angle. Stand up and then repeat the movement. Be sure to keep your torso straight and your shoulders back.

2. Lunges

Lunges help improve hip mobility and strengthen your thigh muscles. Both of these are extremely important for developing the ability to tread for the duration of the game.

There are several variations of the lunge exercise and among the most common is the forward lunge, which begins with your feet positioned hip-width apart and your hands on your hips.

Take one long step forward and then bend the knee of your forward foot until the one at the back slightly touches the ground. Rise and return to starting position. Repeat the movement with your other leg. Be sure to keep your torso upright.

3. Jumps

Jumps provide you with an excellent way to develop explosive power for water polo. These exercises are perhaps the fastest and best way to work your thigh muscles. It's best to do ten repetitions in two to three sets. Basic jumps are performed with your legs hip-width apart.

Bend your legs at a comfortable level and then explode upwards, jumping as high as you can. Bring your knees towards your chest and then land softly with your knees bent to prepare for another jump. You may use your arms to achieve more height.

4. Wall Sits

This exercise is done by sitting with your back against the wall such that your thighs are held parallel to the ground. Your shins and thighs should be at a 90-degree angle.

Keep your knees close and hold the position for about 30 seconds to start with. If you want to challenge yourself even more, squeeze a ball between your knees. Be sure not to brace your arms against your legs and keep your head and chest up at all times.

Adding these exercises to your training routines for water polo can indeed be extremely beneficial, but you'll have to do them diligently. Bear in mind that it a lot easier to get injured when you're on land, so you have to make sure you do these exercises with proper form at all times.

Remember as well that dry land training is meant to be a supplement to practice in water, rather than a replacement.

Water Polo Offense

Offense is defined as a strategy for advancing the ball and then shooting it into the opposing team's goal.

Take note that every player on the team is required to play offense in the sport of water polo. Yes, that includes the goalkeeper.

If you fail to do your part in the offensive play, you'll be exposing your team to pressure, since the opposing team will see you as someone who's not a threat to their own play.

Scoring is obviously the main objective of your offensive play and the strategy you use is generally determined by your coach.

As a beginner in the sport, it's important for you to familiarize the most important aspects of offensive play in water polo.

1. **Protecting Possession**
    You should never make bad passes. Whenever you find yourself near the ball, you need to help your teammates when they come under pressure. You need to always be on the lookout for a good entry pass to the goal.

2. **Advancing the Ball**

   You have to be sure you're close enough to the goal of the opposing team before you attempt a shot.

   Unless you're able to advance the ball effectively, you aren't likely to deliver good offense and you'll probably use up your shot clock just trying to get the ball near the goal.

3. **Creating Fast Break Opportunities**

   You need to anticipate turnovers by your opponents and take active part in a quick counterattack. Whenever you find a good opportunity to shoot, you should take it.

   Otherwise, you should actively protect your possession and make sure a good counterattack is organized.

   When there are more attackers than defenders in front of the cage, you're likely to find a good shooting opportunity.

4. **Transitioning into Organized Front Court Offense in the Absence of Fast Break Opportunities**

You should move the ball into a safe area and pass it so you can possibly open shooting opportunities.

5. **Committing the Defense**
   If you find yourself unguarded at any time, you should move into a good shooting position as quickly as you can and then take the shot.

6. **Creating High-percentage Shot Opportunities**
   Always be on the lookout for mismatches and defensive confusion so you can capitalize on them and initiate plays. You also need to develop the ability to make quick decisions.

   Learn how to recognise where the best shooting opportunity is so you can take the ball there. If you're the one with the best vantage point, then by all means, take the shot. Make every shot count.

Earlier it was mentioned that even the goalkeeper is involved in offense. You may be wondering how.

Bear in mind that the goalkeeper is in the best position to view the entire playing field. He is therefore better able to read the game situation as it develops.

Considering this, he can often be the best person on the team to start offensive play.

If you happen to block, steal, or retrieve the ball from the back court, it's generally advisable to pass it to your goalkeeper so he can initiate the offense. You and the other field players should then get to the front court as quickly as you can.

Defense

There are generally two main objectives for defensive play in water polo.

The first is to prevent the opposing team from scoring goals.

The second is to steal the ball from the other team.

Although the objectives are pretty straightforward, achieving them involves a lot of subtleties in terms of strategy, guarding specific players, and fouling.

Learning the fundamentals of body positioning, keeping track of the ball, and observing other players all at the same time should prepare you for more complex manoeuvres in the future.

The position of your body plays a significant role in determining your effectiveness as a defender. If an offender easily succeeds in swimming around you to receive a pass or advance to the goal, then you're adopting the wrong position.

Regardless of where you are in the playing field, or which player you're guarding, these guidelines should apply:

1. Hips Up

You need to keep your eggbeaters strong when you're defending. Keeping your hips up allows you to change position quickly whenever the need arises. This also allows you to pop up easily to block a shot or intercept a pass. You can also be more easily turned when you let your hips drop and your start on a counterattack is likely to be much less powerful.

2. Defensive Lanes

Getting in a defensive lane means positioning your body such that you get optimal mobility and coverage. Your hips and legs should point in the direction of the goal and your head should always be between the person you're guarding and the ball.

This makes it very difficult for him to receive a pass and enables you to change direction quickly to follow a driver or get back into the hole set.

3. Physical Contact

You should know by now that water polo is essentially a contact sport.

You shouldn't hesitate to keep tabs on whoever you're guarding by resting a hand on their arm, shoulder, or back.

You're not allowed to obstruct them by holding on when they try to move, but keeping your hand on them will certainly make it a bit more uncomfortable for them to make sudden movements. Furthermore, it gives you fair warning as to when they'll be making a move.

When you're tasked to defend the hole, then you're definitely up for some real challenge. After all, this position is the one with the best vantage point to the goal. Needless to say, you should be an extremely strong player in order to successfully play in this position.

Take note that offensive action largely occurs around the hole. This makes it highly important for you to have enough endurance, to prepare for a highly physical play, and to know exactly when and how to foul.

Bear in mind that more grabbing and fighting occurs in this position than in any other area of the playing field, so you really need to be prepared for some rough play.

You need to let your teammates know if you need any help or if you've changed the defensive strategy.

Injury Prevention

Water polo is one sport that's highly physically demanding. It requires you to tread water for the duration of the entire match.

You aren't allowed to stand or hang on to the poolside. Where injuries are concerned, water polo is regarded as a low-risk sport.

Nevertheless, there are some risks and you will have to protect yourself from the common injuries associated with the game, which include the following:

- Eye irritation due to pool chemicals like chlorine.

- Overuse injuries in the hips or knees due to constant treading.

- Shoulder injuries such as strains and sprains.

- Scratches from the fingernails of other players. You may also suffer abrasions, bruises, and cuts as you wrestle for the ball during a match.

- Facial injuries like a split lip or a black eye resulting from physical contact during the game.

- Hypothermia resulting from prolonged exposure to cold conditions.

- Sunburn caused by playing outdoors without sun protection.

- Warts resulting from a viral infection. One of the known risk factors for warts is the use of public swimming pools.

Some of the most common risk factors for water polo injury are the following:

- **Lack of physical fitness**
  If you have poor stamina and lack flexibility, then you're definitely more likely to become injured when playing water polo or any other sport for that matter.

- **Lack of experience**
  Beginners in the sport are likely to lack the necessary skills that will allow them to meet the physical demands of water polo, thus being more prone to injury.

- **Poor technique**
  Without the right technique, your muscles and joints are more likely to suffer from unnecessary strain. Poor technique often leads to awkward shooting and poor throwing action.

- **Lack of protective gear**
  When you neglect to wear protective gear like mouth guards, ear guards, and a swim cap, your risk for injury increases.

To keep yourself safe when playing water polo, it's best to follow these pieces of advice:

- Strictly observe game rules.

- Always work at maintaining proper form. Practice each skill and seek advice from your coach as regards improving your technique and reducing your risk for injury.

- Wear the necessary protective gear.

- Always clip your fingernails and toenails before a game.

- Apply water-resistant sunscreen whenever you play outdoors. Remember to reapply the sunscreen whenever there's a break in the game.

What if you do get injured? Here are the things you should do in case you get injured in any way:

- Stop immediately and ask for substitution so as to prevent further damage.

- Seek immediate treatment. Managing the injury early one often reduces your time away from the game.

- Treat any injury involving soft tissues with ice, elevation, compression, and plenty of rest. Of course, you should also seek the advice of a qualified health professional.

- Don't resume activity (particularly those related to the sport) until you've completely recovered.

Always remember that water polo is a physically demanding game, which requires muscular strength and endurance from any player.

Therefore, you should work on building both strength and endurance so as to avoid injury in water polo.

Nutrition Tips

Water polo naturally involves a lot of swimming, treading, wrestling, and ball throwing. Because of this, it's very important for players to maintain high energy levels.

Knowing when and what to eat is therefore one of the key factors in terms of harnessing your full potential in the sport.

This section provides you with some basic guidelines on the proper nutrition for water polo.

Pre-practice

It's very important to fuel your body before you engage in water polo practice sessions. Take a snack or a light meal an hour or two before practice starts.

This gives your body enough time to digest your food and helps you avoid feeling too full as you start moving around in the pool. Choose foods that are substantial yet easy on the stomach.

Your intake should be limited to 200-400 calories, ideally with a 40-30-30 carbohydrates-protein-fat ratio. Carbohydrates are broken down and used for energy whereas protein helps in muscle-building and provides you with stamina.

Fats then slow down digestion, so you'll have sufficient energy for the entire duration of practice. A good balance allows you to avoid potentially harmful spikes and dips in energy.

Practice Time

In the course of practice, what's important is for you to manage hydration and your blood sugar level.

Since all water polo games and a good deal of practices are held in the water, you probably won't realize just how much you sweat in the process.

Bear in mind that dehydration has a hugely negative effect on your performance, your recovery time, and even on your appearance.

This is why you need to stay hydrated during practice and games by having a water bottle prepared at poolside and then taking regular sips.

And even when you're away from the playing field, you should continue drinking plenty of water.

Additionally, you should remember that blood sugar level changes as your glucose levels change. Sometimes glucose levels can drop so low that it leads to a dramatic drop in your energy level as well.

If you notice that your energy level always drops after a certain period of time, you may want to consider adding carbohydrates and electrolytes to your drink so as to maintain a healthy blood sugar level.

You may also leave an energy bar or gel beside your water bottle to get a mid-practice energy boost.

Post-practice

Eating right after a training session gives you an extra energy boost to help you go on with the rest of your day.

Furthermore, it helps your body restore and rebuild the muscles that have just been broken down through hours of practice.

Your 'recovery' meal or snack should be eaten within one hour after your practice session. This is the time when your body can replenish its stores of energy most efficiently, so you can be sure of turning your food into muscle instead of fat.

It's best to take in a 100-200 calorie snack comprised by a three-to-one carbohydrate-protein ratio.

You should also remember that adequate rest is just as important as food in enhancing the recovery process.

76630028R00058

Made in the USA
San Bernardino, CA
13 May 2018